SECRETS

To Get Busy People To Respond To Your Messages

66 Tips to Compelling

⇨ Letters
⇨ E-mail
⇨ Proposals
⇨ Presentations

Bonnie Budzowski, MA

W9-CYB-299

*For Joy and the coach
behind the coach.*

You mean the world to me.

Copyright 2004 by WordCoach™, LP
All rights reserved. No part of this book may be
reproduced in any form, except for brief reviews, without
written permission from the publisher. For permission,
contact Bonnie Budzowski at www.wordcoach.biz.

Copies of this book are available at a quantity discount.
To order one or more additional copies, contact Bonnie
Budzowski at www.wordcoach.biz.

TABLE OF CONTENTS

Introduction   7

**What Can You Do to Make Your
Messages Stand Out?**   11

**The Central Tip: Make All Your
Communication About the Receiver**   15

    Design Every Message from the
    Receiver's Point of View   19

    Structure Your Messages to Make
    Things Easy for the Receiver   27

    Make Your Messages Visually
    Attractive and Accessible   35

    Be Strategically Concise   43

    Use Your Style and Voice to Make
    Things Easy for the Receiver   51

    Think of Your Messages in Their
    Larger Context   59

Review   69

Where to Go From Here   71

Resources   73

INTRODUCTION

INTRODUCTION

Even your most important messages face stiff competition.

The information age has served us well and served us poorly at the same time. It's great to have information available at the click of a mouse. Yet, to some extent, many of us feel like we are drowning in a sea of information. The sea includes reports and presentations that contain unnecessary data just because the data is available; messages we receive from co-workers who are indiscriminate about distribution lists; and messages that result from *reply all* frenzies.

We've reached a point of information exhaustion. We neither want nor have the ability to respond to the avalanche of e-mail, hard copy mailings, and multi-media messages that compete for our attention. A large percentage of electronic and printed messages sent our way end up deleted or tossed. Most of the presentations we attend receive our partial attention, at best.

Unfortunately, a large percentage of the documents we send and the presentations we give—even the important ones—suffer the same fate.

WHAT CAN YOU DO TO MAKE YOUR MESSAGES STAND OUT?

Life is a series of sales situations. You sell your ideas, value, and point of view daily.

Patricia Fripp,
Fripp News

What Can You Do to Make Your Messages Stand Out?

Think of every message as a marketing task.

Think of your messages in this way because the messages you send are, in fact, attempts to persuade. Sometimes the attempt is obvious. For example, presentations to seek approval for funds and ads to promote products are obviously intended to be persuasive. Yet, to be successful as professionals, even our most mundane messages must persuade others to do the following:

- Open and read our e-mail messages

- Supply information we need to do our jobs

- Comply with department or company procedures

- Respect our expertise

- Support our position for a specific solution

- Compensate us for our contributions

Our daily messages are, by nature, persuasive. We must think of them—all of them—in terms of marketing. If we want our messages to be noticed in an oncoming sea of information, even to leap out at our intended receivers, we must be strategic about the messages.

The point of this book is to change the way you think about your daily messages. It describes proven tips to

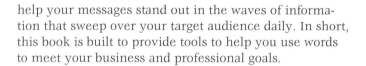

help your messages stand out in the waves of information that sweep over your target audience daily. In short, this book is built to provide tools to help you use words to meet your business and professional goals.

THE CENTRAL TIP:
MAKE YOUR COMMUNICATION
ALL ABOUT THE RECEIVER

[T]he main advice of this book: think constantly about your readers.

Paul Anderson,
Technical Writing

THE CENTRAL TIP:
MAKE YOUR COMMUNICATION
ALL ABOUT THE RECEIVER

When you learned to communicate as a child, the whole process was about you. You were learning and being evaluated for your use of language, punctuation, and vocabulary. Your teacher, although he or she may have marked your pages with a red pen, actually cared about you and what you wrote. That same teacher, when pointing out your mistakes, cared about what you had to say.

Things are entirely different in your professional world. Things are no longer about you. Busy people care about your messages only in relation to how the messages matter to them—to *their* goals, priorities, and schedules. If you expect someone to pay attention to what you write or say, make sure the message is all about the receiver.

This tip is foundational to everything else in this book.

Make your messages receiver-focused, and your communication will automatically get better results.

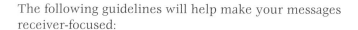

The following guidelines will help make your messages receiver-focused:

- ✍ **Design every message from the receiver's point of view**

- ✍ **Structure your messages to make things easy for the receiver**

- ✍ **Make your messages visually attractive and accessible**

- ✍ **Be strategically concise**

- ✍ **Use your style and voice to make things easy for the receiver**

- ✍ **Think of your messages in their larger context**

Note:

Since the term *receiver* applies to readers and listeners alike, it will be used to refer to both throughout this book.

DESIGN EVERY MESSAGE FROM THE RECEIVER'S POINT OF VIEW

An exceptional business presentation, written or spoken, weaves an intricate connection between the speaker's recommendation and the decision-maker's goals.

–Bonnie Budzowski

DESIGN EVERY MESSAGE FROM THE RECEIVER'S POINT OF VIEW

1. **Think of your reader or listener as a customer.**

   Whether the message is internal or external to your organization, think about what you are selling. It might be a new product line, a solution to a long-standing problem, your credibility as a professional, or your firm as the top supplier.

   Even messages that seem purely informational have persuasive themes.

   For example, if you send a memo outlining changes in the procedure for filing expense reports, you want readers to save the information and use it to prepare future expense reports.

   Your message must be designed to "sell" the reader on taking the time to understand the new procedures, to have them on hand at the appropriate time, and to use them.

2. **Connect your message to your receiver's priorities.**

   People sort incoming messages, consciously or unconsciously, in terms of priorities or hot buttons. Identify the receiver's priorities and points of frustration before you write or speak. Do formal or informal research, if necessary, to identify these points. Design your pages and presentations to make an obvious connection between the reader's priorities and your message or recommendation.

While receiver priorities are critical to all effective communication, pay special attention to them when developing proposals or executive reports and presentations. In these situations, receivers are especially unwilling to attend to messages that are not clearly related to their priorities.

3.   Anticipate the receiver's objections.

Make sure your research includes identifying the receiver's potential objections—those that are logical and those that are not. Address these obstacles before they cause the receiver to reject your message. You can address objections directly or indirectly, depending on the situation, but get those objections out of the way.

4.   Know your receiver's preference.

Some people, including some decision-makers, don't like e-mail. Others want nothing but e-mail. Some people like a piece of paper to review; others like to brainstorm about a problem face-to-face. If you hope to catch someone's attention, intentionally use his or her preferred venue of communication, not your own.

5.   Resist the temptation to impress.

Get rid of writing habits you used to impress your middle school teacher. Long documents with

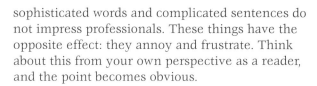

sophisticated words and complicated sentences do not impress professionals. These things have the opposite effect: they annoy and frustrate. Think about this from your own perspective as a reader, and the point becomes obvious.

Audience members want an intelligent presentation that answers their questions. Avoid frustrating them with unnecessary details designed to impress rather than to inform. Get to the point and be done. When appropriate, provide resources on the technical details.

6.   **Transform the urge to impress.**

Turn the urge to impress into a commitment to serve the receiver. If your message is relevant and helpful to the receiver, you increase the odds of capturing the receiver's attention and meeting your own goals.

7.   **Begin with gusto.**

It takes a receiver a matter of seconds to form an impression—to decide to listen to or read your message, discount it, or ignore it altogether. Don't waste precious opening seconds with banalities like, "Thanks for the opportunity to describe our qualifications." Start with a bang, like, "Our approach to your project will shave 20% off your operating costs."

EXAMPLE OF I-CENTERED AND YOU-CENTERED WRITING

"I" Centered Version:

I have experience as a recruiter in a large institution, a specialist in a job-readiness program, and in other positions in human resources. My experience points to a need for a quick, easy-to-read guide of tips people can use in their job searches. I wrote this book for job seekers to share my experiences to help make their job searches go more smoothly.

"You" Centered Version:

The purpose of this book is to make your job search easier, less frustrating, and more successful.

This book is a quick, easy-to-read guide you can use for any job search. It's based on my experiences as a recruiter. You'll find tips about things that worked and things that haven't worked—in job searches of real people. Follow this guide for an easier, less frustrating, and more successful path to your new job!

8.   Check your I/You ratio.

Make sure you couch your message more in terms of "you" and the name of the customer (internal or external) than in terms of "I" or the name of your firm. To check yourself on this, simply count and make a ratio of "I" words versus "you" words. The higher the focus on "you," the more likely you are to catch and keep the receiver's attention. Check the sidebar for an example.

International speaker and sales coach, Patricia Fripp, credits this tip as an item of strong perceived value by her clients. PSMJ, a large marketing consulting firm to the design and construction industry, emphasizes this point as well.

9.   Think of what motivates your receivers to act.

In *The Copywriter's Handbook,* expert Robert Bly lists 22 reasons people buy products. These same motivators are behind people buying ideas and approaches. People buy ideas and make decisions for some of the following reasons: to be liked, to feel important, to make money, to save money, to make work easier, to be secure, to be distinct, for convenience, out of fear, and out of greed.

10. Identify benefits to the receiver.

Avoid a focus on features or characteristics of your product, proposal, or approach. Focus on benefits to the receiver, based on what motivates that receiver.

For example, if you recommend outsourcing an administrative function in your office, avoid focusing on the services of the firm you want to hire. Focus on the results or benefits the office will receive with outsourcing: convenience, time, and dollars saved. Some talk of features is usually necessary, but focus on the benefits.

Be as specific and quantitative about the benefits as possible.

11. Revise from the receiver's point of view.

Once you've completed a written draft or a presentation outline, get away from it for awhile. When you come back, make your first step to review the message from the receiver's vantage point. Both the break and the vantage point will help you see the message differently. The longer the break you take, the better the perspective you'll get. Adjust accordingly.

STRUCTURE YOUR MESSAGES TO MAKE THINGS EASY FOR THE RECEIVER

STRUCTURE YOUR MESSAGES TO MAKE THINGS EASY FOR THE RECEIVER

12. Use a strategic subject line.

☞ In e-mail, use the subject line to identify yourself, a specific subject, or benefits that are relevant to the reader. Write a subject line that will distinguish your message from the avalanche of e-mail this person receives. Be clear, not cute.

☞ In memos, and even in formal letters, use a subject line to quickly clarify the subject of the message. This technique is acceptable and useful in today's business climate. It helps the reader make an immediate determination about the importance or urgency of the message.

13. Clarify the purpose of your message.

A busy person wants to start out knowing why he or she is reading or listening. Will the message do one of the following?

☞ Provide information the reader needs to know?

☞ Provide support for a specific perspective, project, position, or solution?

☞ Require a decision or action from the reader?

When you are clear about your purpose, you are more likely to get the response you want.

14. Provide an overview or skeleton of your message.

Any document or talk, even a short one, provides chunks and pieces of information. Identifying your organizational structure is like providing the picture on the box top of a jigsaw puzzle. It makes it much easier for the receiver to see how the pieces fit together.

15. State your conclusion or recommendation early.

A busy receiver is unwilling to wade through text or endure a long presentation to get to the point. Stating the conclusion early gets the receiver's attention and allows him or her to focus on what's important. It also helps the receiver to follow your logic and see how the supporting information fits together.

16. Make your points in descending order of importance—from the receiver's perspective.

A reader might get interrupted and never get back to your document. A listener might get distracted or called out of your audience. If you grab the receiver's attention at the beginning, you increase the chances that he or she will stick with or return to your message.

Managers at every level are prisoners of the notion that a simple style reflects a simple mind. Actually, a simple style is the result of hard work and hard thinking; a muddled style reflects a muddled thinker or a person too arrogant, or too dumb, or too lazy to organize his thoughts.

William Zinsser,
On Writing Well

17. Avoid needlessly complicating your point.

Say what you have to say plainly and directly. This shortens your sentences, makes the message personal, and makes the message easier to follow. As a result, the receiver feels like he or she is receiving information rather than enduring it.

18. Make key information easy to identify.

Save a receiver time and frustration in looking for relevant information. For example, if you are announcing an event, make it simple for the receiver to find the date, time, location, and cost involved.

Support presentations with slides or handouts that reinforce key information, rather than document everything in the presentation. Also change your tone of voice and use strategic pauses to reinforce key points.

MAKE YOUR MESSAGES VISUALLY ATTRACTIVE AND ACCESSIBLE

MAKE YOUR MESSAGES VISUALLY ATTRACTIVE AND ACCESSIBLE

19. Keep it light and white.

Use plenty of white or blank space to keep your pages or slides from appearing dense and uninviting. An abundance of words actually de-emphasizes your key points. White space highlights them.

20. Expect your documents to be scanned rather than read.

It's discouraging to think a reader will only scan a document that you've carefully written, but this, unfortunately, is the treatment you should expect. There's nothing personal in this—it's the result both of information overload and the way human comprehension works.

Humans don't read pages word-by-word, but by an involuntary scanning process that looks at the whole.

Use this knowledge to your advantage: Use headings in a way that someone scanning the document will catch your whole message at first glance. If the headlines are relevant and compelling, they will draw the scanner into the document.

21. Learn the most basic principles of graphic design.

You don't need an intensive knowledge of graphic arts to produce an attractive page or slide. You can learn what you need in most situations from Robin

BASIC PRINCIPLES OF GRAPHIC DESIGN

Contrast

When you choose to vary elements (FONT, color, size, line thickness, shape, etc.), make the difference obvious. Similar elements do not work well together.

Repetition

Repeat visual items (FONT, color, size, line thickness, shape, etc.) throughout the piece. This reinforces the organization of the piece and creates a unified look.

Alignment

Make sure every element has some visual connection with another element on the page. For example, the box surrounding a graphic should line up with text or some other graphic on the page.

Proximity

Place items that relate to each together in a group. In other words, use space to create visual units of text. This helps organize information and reduce clutter.

Adapted from Robin Williams, *The Non-Designer's Design Book*.

Williams' helpful book, *The Non-Designer's Design Book*. This book is worth the investment, and it is fun to read. Before and after examples make the points clear at a glance. For a brief overview of Williams's four design principles, see the sidebar.

22. **Make your headings tell and sell the message.**

Most people rely on topical headings, and they rely on them primarily to show the hierarchy of their material. Go farther with headings and help the receiver catch your message at first glance. If you use headlines well, they will draw the receiver into the details of the message.

For example, instead of using a topical heading like *Population* in a document or slide, make the heading carry a conclusion: *Population in Dangerous Decline.* When possible, make the heading describe a benefit, and the message becomes even more compelling: *Declining Population Presents Business Opportunity.*

23. **Expect your slides to upstage you.**

Be aware that visuals are powerful, and your slides can work like a magnet to draw attention away from you. Develop your slides so they support you rather than upstage you.

Use slides to emphasize your key points, and use slides as a way to visualize a product, a process, or a startling statistic. Use slides, *but use them sparingly,* and *keep them simple.* Avoid giving the audience the opportunity to read things on a slide that would be more dynamic coming from you.

If you are the speaker, keep control of the presentation.

24. Use bullets or numbered lists.

These formats break text up visually and increase white space. Bullets are helpful to someone scanning a document or slide. Even for a careful receiver, bullets show how concepts or points are related.

25. Take time to learn features of your software.

Many people use their word processors as typewriters. This is under-utilizing the capacity of a powerful tool. Word processing programs have simple commands that can help you format pages to make specific things jump off the page. Invest time in learning to use your word processor as a tool to distinguish your pages. Invest time in learning PowerPoint to distinguish your slides.

26. Think of visual variety as the spice of life.

Use images, graphics, text boxes, and quotes to add interest and to break up text. When possible, use a visual element to make your meaning clear at a glance. When done well, pictures and graphics draw receivers into your message.

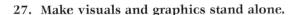

27. Make visuals and graphics stand alone.

Visuals attract attention, even from readers and audience members who have neither time nor intention to give their full attention to your message. In some cases, the visuals are the only chance to tell your story. Make sure those visuals can tell the story by themselves.

28. Label all visuals and graphics.

Use labels and captions to direct readers and viewers to your meaning. Do not assume your message is self-evident. Facts and data can be interpreted in many different ways. Your captions improve the chances the receiver will interpret your story as you intend.

29. Conquer clutter.

Clean and simple lines make pages and slides inviting. Busy graphics are confusing and annoying. Busy screens, with an extensive variety of font sizes and styles, repel the eye.

30. Use Color.

To the extent you have the capacity, use color to attract attention and show the structure of your document or presentation. Remember to be simple and tasteful with your colors. Color clutter is still clutter.

31. Avoid typing in all capital letters.

The human eye reads via shapes of words, so documents and slides in all capital letters are difficult to read. In e-mail messages, using all capital letters comes off as shouting.

BE STRATEGICALLY CONCISE

People expect to run through their e-mail like a bowl of pistachio nuts. And you know what happens to the ones that are hard to open.

Sarah Myers McGinty,
Power Talk

BE STRATEGICALLY CONCISE

32. Strive for one.

Discipline yourself to think in terms of one-page letters and one-screen e-mail messages. The shorter your message, the more likely the reader will attend to your message *now*, rather than place it aside or delete it.

33. Stick to one.

Limit yourself to one message per e-mail or memo. People prefer to read several short e-mail messages, each on its own topic, rather than one long e-mail.

34. Provide a killer executive summary.

Begin any proposal or report with a stand-alone overview directed to the decision-maker(s). Spend a considerable amount of preparation time to make this section attractive, easy to scan, and targeted to the reader(s). Clearly connect your recommendation to the decision-maker's goals and priorities. Focus on benefits.

Follow the same principles to begin a presentation with a killer overview. This gets the presentation off to a dynamic start. It also helps the audience put subsequent details into perspective.

Nonprofessional writers are relieved when they've been able to produce an abundance of words—and they try hard to keep them. Professionals, on the other hand, are pleased to find how many they can cut in successive revisions. There are undoubtedly more precise ways to separate the professional from the nonprofessional writer, but this difference in attitude toward quantity is certainly significant.

Theodore Cheney,
Getting the Words Right

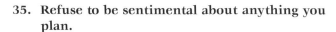

35. Refuse to be sentimental about anything you plan.

If an explanation, a story, or a chart isn't relevant or of interest *from the receiver's perspective*, get rid of it (or file it for future use). The more words you subtract, the more likely you are to get readers to pay attention to what you say. Make subtracting words a habit, and your communication will get better results.

36. Use a one-sentence paragraph.

Chances are a teacher told you a one-sentence paragraph is against grammatical rules. Don't worry, you aren't in school anymore! Fiction writers and professional copywriters use one-sentence paragraphs routinely. A one-sentence paragraph, *used sparingly,* sticks out. This is because it is surrounded by white space.

37. Cultivate a strategic pause.

A pause serves as white space in a verbal presentation. Use a pause to emphasize key points and give the audience time to absorb them.

38. Layer and link your material.

When one page is genuinely insufficient for your message, consider a light, attractive introductory page which shows the reader how to find more details. These details can be in text that follows, in appendices, or in web links. Bruce Ross-Larson, in *Writing for the Information Age*, advises that you design all messages to be light, layered, and linked.

39. Perform a background check.

In creating a proposal, project report, or technical presentation, discipline yourself to limit the background to what the receiver genuinely needs. It's tempting to provide a full chronological background and/or context for your project. If you do this, you risk losing the receiver's attention before he or she even gets to the point.

40. Present your material in short chunks.

Short sentences and short paragraphs make your writing and speaking easier to digest. Author Theodore Cheney reports that people scan as they read, their thoughts moving at about 200 mph. Paragraph breaks, and even periods, give the eye a needed rest. Cheney represents this concept in an equation: white space = time = emphasis.

41. Think of revising as more than tweaking.

Adjusting a few words and checking punctuation is not revising. It's tweaking. To revise means to *re-vision*, to step back and take a fresh look at what

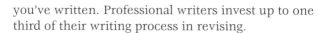

you've written. Professional writers invest up to one third of their writing process in revising.

42. Don't revise your writing until it is time to revise.

Separate your writing process into phases: planning, writing, and revising. Refuse to correct or revise any sentence until you've completed a first draft. If you haven't spent time correcting the material, you are less likely to be sentimental about it.

43. Don't revise your presentation until it is time to revise.

As you prepare your presentation, separate the work into phases: generating material, structuring material, and rehearsing. You may run through these three steps several times, but it saves time to keep them as separate and distinct steps.

44. Once you say, "in conclusion," conclude.

Once you signal that you intend to finish your remarks, the listeners expect the message to end. They stop listening, so make sure you stop talking.

USE YOUR STYLE AND VOICE TO MAKE THINGS EASY FOR THE RECEIVER

A legendary anecdote reports than an American general once asked Winston Churchill to read the draft of a speech. "Too many passives and too many zeds," Churchill commented. Asked to explain his comment, Churchill said:

> Too many Latinate polysyllables like "systematize, prioritize, finalize." And then the passives. What if I had said—instead of "We shall fight on the beaches"— "Hostilities will be engaged with our adversaries on the coastal perimeter?"

Richard Lanham,
Revising Prose

USE YOUR STYLE AND VOICE TO MAKE THINGS EASY FOR THE RECEIVER

45. Write and present conversationally.

In the past, readers expected professional writing to have a lofty, distant, and stuffy tone, like "pursuant to the above-mentioned matter...." Sentence after sentence of such language is both dull and difficult for readers. It makes the reader want to put the document down, move to another electronic message, or take a nap.

In a presentation, a relaxed and personal tone helps you make a strong connection with the audience. This is vital to the success of your message.

46. Use short, normal words.

It's tempting to use impressive words to try to build credibility. If you have a sophisticated concept that requires a precise technical term, use it; otherwise, stick to simple, straightforward words. This tip is whimsically illustrated in the following interchange between Owl, Pooh, and Christopher Robin:

> "The atmospheric conditions have been very unfavorable lately," said Owl.

> "The what?" asked Pooh.

> "It's been raining," offered Christopher Robin.

Saturate your audience with eye contact.

Granville N. Toogood,
The Articulate Executive

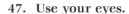

47. Use your eyes.

It's impossible to overestimate the importance of
strong eye contact in both face-to-face conversations
and presentations. Make sure you really look into the
eyes of the people to whom you are speaking. This
helps listeners stay engaged and feel connected to
you. Most importantly, good eye contact causes the
audience to perceive you as a trustworthy individual.

48. Connect with your readers emotionally as well as logically.

Successful communicators know that people make
decisions both on a gut and an intellectual level.
Receivers are often unaware how much weight they
give to gut feeling. At the very least, be sure to show
an emotional commitment to your idea, solution, or
product. This doesn't mean you need to be overly
dramatic. Match the emotion in your communication to a level appropriate to the situation.

49. Remove barriers between you and your audience.

Get rid of anything that creates distance between
you and your audience. This includes podiums,
tables, and wordy slides.

Wordy slides create a conflict for audience members
who must decide whether to read the slides or listen to
you. Because slides are visual, the slides usually win.

Nearly every American has some recognition of Martin Luther King Jr.'s great *I Have a Dream* speech, delivered nearly 40 years ago. The speech captured a deep longing for justice and equality among both blacks and whites. It connected with people emotionally. The speech also painted a series of specific, vivid pictures that envisioned a better future in America. Here are two excerpts:

> "I have a dream that one day on the red hills of Georgia, sons of former slaves and sons of former slave-owners will be able to sit down together at the table of brotherhood."

> "I have a dream my four little children will one day live in a nation where they will not be judged by the color of their skin but by the content of their character."

Most of us don't write or present about subjects as deeply stirring as freedom. Even so, we communicate to people about things they care about, even if the subject is choosing the best solution to a problem. We can make our messages more compelling by painting specific and vivid pictures.

50. Paint pictures with your words.

When you ask a reader or listener to respond to a story, imagine a scenario, or envision a future, that person participates in the message. When the receiver participates in your message, he or she remains interested and engaged. People find vivid images and examples both interesting and memorable.

51. Be specific.

Even professional communicators produce first drafts and speaking points that are full of vague and abstract points. Since vague messages can be both bland and easily misinterpreted, invest the time needed to clarify what you mean.

Specificity breeds interest and clarity. Use examples, case studies, analogies, and statistics. Just remember to use the statistics sparingly. A few dramatic statistics can be compelling. As the number of statistical examples grows, the dramatic effect decreases.

52. Don't just plan your presentation; rehearse it— out loud!

Don't feel silly about rehearsing your presentation out loud, and don't neglect this crucial step. When possible, rehearse your presentation in the room in which you will deliver it.

53. Use your imagination.

Professional speakers prepare much like professional athletes do. They plan, they practice, and they envision their success.

Imagine yourself connecting successfully with the audience. Not only will this process help you find mistakes and awkward spots, it will increase your confidence. Confidence is a key factor in getting people to respond to your message.

THINK OF YOUR MESSAGES IN THEIR LARGER CONTEXT

Credibility is determined by expertise and relationship. Before you try to persuade, make an honest assessment of **how others perceive you** on both criteria. Try this approach:

Ask yourself questions about your perceived expertise:

What do others think about my knowledge surrounding the strategy, product, or change I am proposing? Do I have a respected track record in this area?

Ask yourself questions about the strength of your relationships:

Do the people I hope to persuade see me as helpful, trustworthy, and supportive? Do these people see me as a person in harmony with them on an emotional, intellectual, and political level—concerning this kind of issue?

Once you've completed your self-assessment, check with a few colleagues to see if their perceptions match yours. This is a check to help you see the situation objectively.

Adapted from Jay A. Conger, The Necessary Art of Persuasion in *Harvard Business Review*

THINK OF YOUR MESSAGES IN THEIR LARGER CONTEXT

54. Appreciate the value of relationship.

People pay attention to others whom they trust. Make a commitment to build trust before, during, and after the message.

Sales guru, Jeffrey Gitomer said something like this, "People don't like to be sold, but they do like to buy. They like to buy from people they trust." This statement describes how people feel about buying ideas or approving projects within an organization as well as how they feel about buying major services from competing vendors.

55. Think long-term.

Build long-term relationships both inside and outside your organization. Show interest in people's priorities, projects, and families. Stay in touch. When you need a person's attention, a positive history is priceless.

56. Become a resource for others.

Be creative in how you share information. Make sure you, your department, or your business provides free information to any extent possible. Create a newsletter or direct people to free information on your website. Intentionally share links and resources. You can view an example of a free electronic newsletter at www.wordcoach.biz. For another example, see www.coloringoutsidethelines.com.

Do something that says, "I took the time to get to know you...."

Jeffrey Gitomer,
The Sales Bible

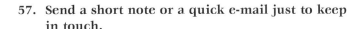

57. Send a short note or a quick e-mail just to keep in touch.

Notice things that impact others, and let them know you notice. For example, celebrate the successes of your colleagues. Acknowledge birthdays and new babies.

Joanne Sujansky, successful speaker on an international scale, sends an average of six personal notes a day. This is time well-invested. It is time that pays back.

58. Send an article, link, or business lead.

Make a habit of clipping or forwarding valuable information. Read newspapers, magazines, journals, and online sources with others in mind.

59. Send postcards.

While the time involved in writing a personal postcard is negligible, the results in goodwill are high.

Printed postcards get a lot of mileage, too. This is because people judge a letter by its *envelope*. They open a letter or toss it based on this judgment. Since a postcard doesn't have an envelope, people glance at it, even if they are carrying it toward the trash.

In our writing workshops, the most frequent complaint about e-mail is this lament: "I get so much stuff that I just delete a lot without reading them. And in doing that, I probably miss things I should have read." Then these attendees go on to call names of people and departments that send e-mail to them for which they have no interest and often do not understand.

Dianna Booher, *E-Writing: 21st-Century Tools for Effective Communication*

60. Be consistently considerate about what you send.

If you avoid wasting people's time with unwanted messages, they are more likely to read what you send. Avoid sending junk mail of any kind.

Here are a few simple rules:

☞ Limit copies of meeting minutes to those who genuinely need them.

☞ Don't use your *reply all* key unless it makes sense for all recipients to read the message you are sending.

☞ Don't send inspirational e-mail messages or jokes unless you are absolutely certain the person wants to receive them.

61. Be consistently considerate about what you say.

Words that offend or wound are not easily forgotten. When a person uses offensive words in public presentations or around the office water cooler, the best case scenario is that the person loses credibility and attention to his or her serious messages. Don't forget the rules you already know:

☞ Refrain completely from off-color humor.

☞ Refrain completely from insensitive comments about any person, gender, nationality, or group.

62. Don't get lost or forgotten.

Remember the old adage, "out of sight, out of mind." Communicate frequently with important people, at least once per quarter. Choose the most appropriate way to stay in touch, based on the situation. For example, some businesses send a printed postcard to their customers once each quarter.

63. Be persistent.

If you are having trouble getting someone to respond to a message, avoid an automatic assumption that they've rejected you or your message. Many things can prevent a person from responding as you expect.

Strive to achieve a balance between persistence and politeness. Follow up on your message, using different channels. For example, follow an e-mail with a phone call. Follow a phone call with a letter or a personal note.

64. Keep learning and growing.

People listen to experts in their fields. Stay current.

65. Read widely.

A broad body of knowledge helps you to have a broad perspective about issues that impact others. This gives you material to build rapport with

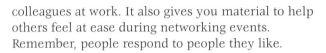

colleagues at work. It also gives you material to help others feel at ease during networking events. Remember, people respond to people they like.

66. **Give free stuff.**

Within proper business guidelines, people love to get stuff for free. Free stuff gets people's attention because it builds good will. I'm not talking here about expensive or elaborate gifts. Try, for example, sharing handout materials from a seminar a colleague was unable to attend.

In seminars I facilitate, I give free fidget toys, especially little slinkys. People are usually surprised about the slinkys and enjoy playing with them.

I love seeing my slinkys in offices I visit months after a seminar. When I see one of those toys on a desk, I know I've built some fun and simple goodwill into a relationship. I know I've caught someone's attention. Next time I send this person an e-mail, he or she is likely to respond. I've met my goal: I caught the attention of a busy person. You can too.

REVIEW, WHERE TO GO FROM HERE, AND RESOURCES

REVIEW

E ven your most important messages face stiff competition. This fact doesn't change if you are the expert. It doesn't change if you have the best solution.

In order to succeed, you have to grab your receiver's attention to convince him or her that taking the time to pay attention to your message is worthwhile. To do this, you must make your message stand out from the sea of information this person receives daily.

The most effective thing you can do is to make your messages—written and verbal—obviously about the receiver. This is the central tip of this book. Nothing works better than thinking like the receiver and delivering what you have to say in a way that serves this person.

Here's a review of the main tips on how to accomplish this:

- **Design every message from the receiver's point of view**

- **Structure your messages to make things easy for the receiver**

- **Make your messages visually attractive and accessible**

- **Be strategically concise**

- **Use your style and voice to make things easy for the receiver**

- **Think of your messages in their larger context**

WHERE TO GO FROM HERE

The tips in this book are not hard to follow. They are, however, contrary to most people's habits. And habits are hard to break. To break a habit requires a commitment to make and stick with small steps toward change.

Use the space below to record the three most personally compelling or valuable tips in this book.

1. _____

2. _____

3. _____

List three to five changes you will make as a result of these tips:

1. _____

2. _____

3. _____

4. _____

5. _____

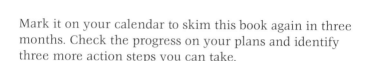

Mark it on your calendar to skim this book again in three months. Check the progress on your plans and identify three more action steps you can take.

Skim this book and create new action steps every three months for a year after you read these tips for the first time. Then, by all means, write or e-mail me (bonnie@wordcoach.biz) to let me know what happened!

Steady steps, taken over time, will transform the way you communicate and the way people respond. You know 66 secrets to get people to respond to your messages. Use these secrets to ensure your messages are distinguished—that they even leap out from a sea of information—to achieve the results you want.

RESOURCES

As noted in the text, some short quotes and adaptations come from the following sources. I'm grateful to these authors for their insights, and I recommend them to you.

Anderson, Paul V. (1995) *Technical Writing: A Reader-Centered Approach,* 3rd edition. Fort Worth: Harcourt Brace Publishers.

Bly, Robert W. (1985) *The Copywriter's Handbook,* Updated edition. New York: Henry Holt and Company.

Booher, Dianna. (2001) *E-Writing: 21st-Century Tools for Effective Communication.* New York: Pocket Books.

Cheney, Theodore A. (1983) *Getting the Words Right: How to Rewrite, Edit & Revise.* Cincinnati: Writer's Digest Books.

Conger, Jay A. (1998) The Necessary Art of Persuasion. *Harvard Business Review,* reprint number 98304.

Gitomer, Jeffrey. (2003) *The Sales Bible.* Hoboken, New Jersey: John Wiley & Sons, Inc.

Lanham, Richard. (2000) *Revising Prose.* Boston: Allyn and Bacon.

McGinty, Sarah Myers. (2001) *PowerTalk.* New York: Warner Books.

Ross-Larson, Bruce. (2002) *Writing for the Information Age.* New York: W.W. Norton & Company.

Toogood, Granville N. (1996) *The Articulate Executive.* New York: McGraw Hill.

Williams, Robin. (1994) *The Non-Designer's Design Book.* Berkeley: Peach Pit Press.

Zinsser, William. (1998) *On Writing Well*, 6th edition. New York: HarperCollins Publishers.

For other WordCoach™, LP resources or to order additional copies of this book, please visit www.wordcoach.biz

NOTES

ABOUT BONNIE BUDZOWSKI, MA

After 20 + years in the communication field, Bonnie remains passionate about the power of words to build success.

Much of Bonnie's work focuses on executives, professionals, and groups who are trained in business or in a technical specialty. She helps people build the skills needed to use daily communication tasks to support their business and career goals.

As founder and principal of WordCoach™, Bonnie provides value to organizations in a variety of venues, both large and small. She works on projects in large organizations, builds ongoing business relationships with principals in smaller firms, and coaches executives and professionals one-on-one.

Bonnie is a qualified member of the National Speakers Association. She is also a member of the Pittsburgh Chapter of The American Society of Training and Development.

Bonnie is author of the *WordCoach™ Free Electronic Newsletter* and a number of nationally published articles.

Choose Bonnie as your performance partner in matching communication tasks to your business or personal goals. You'll begin to think about communication in a whole new, wholly productive way.

Contact Bonnie at bonnie@wordcoach.biz or visit www.wordcoach.biz.